'Ave yer

bin busy?

'Ave yer

bin busy

True tales of a taxi driver

Simon Whiskey

Illustrations by Millie Harrop

In Memoriam.

A.J.C

"Cowboy"

Contents

INTRODUCTION

Dear reader,

There are not many people who at some time of their life have not ridden in a taxi of some sort, be it a black cab, the ubiquitous Skoda Octavia, or ford transit minibus.

Whatever the journey and however infrequent or frequent the usage, the customer always manages to ask the same Chuffing question(s) every time!

I'd like you to try a little experiment

for me. Next time you're in the Bank, or butty shop, or in the pub, or just chatting to the postman, before they have chance to breathe, make sure you ask them if they've been busy, or, if it's going to rain, or, if he's ready for Chrimbo, see what looks you get.

Double check what time they started work and when they expect to finish. You get the picture.

What is it about getting in a taxi that turns everybody over the age of 40 into

the nosiest bastard on earth? They simply
can't help it.

Why only over 40's I hear you ask?
Because generally anyone under that age
is immediately nose deep in an I-phone
and you could take them to Timbuktu via
Blackpool and back and they wouldn't
notice.

Some questions are seasonal as I will
explain shortly, but some are evergreen,
and I'd love to know when the first punter
first asked a cabbie "'Ave yer bin busy?"
and whether he was pleasantly surprised

that the punter cared enough to ask, or,
whether like now, he snorts gently, sighs,
answers the question and resigns himself
to the fact that because in no small part to
Peter fuckin Kay (they asked it before he
came along but he definitely made it
worse) people will ALWAYS ask that
question!

Here's a list of standard questions
dear reader so you can make sure you ask
them all next time you're in the back seat
and really, REALLY want to know the
answers!

1 Have you been busy?

2 What time are you on 'til?

3 What time did you start?

4 Is this your own car?

5 Is it going to rain?

6 Do you have a school run?

7 Have you done any school runs?

8 What's the furthest you've ever been on a job?

9 How long have you been doing taxiing?

10 Do you like being a taxi driver?

Seasonal questions:

From October 'til December 24th

Are you ready for Christmas?

From December 26th 'til February.

Have you had a nice Christmas?

From February to May

Are you going away?

From May through to September.

Have you been away?

See if you can get them all in,

y'know; remember them all as a sort of

personal test, like trying to remember all

the costumes the Village people wore.

Yeah, that's got you thinking, hasn't it?

Bet you said the leather clad p*****r

biker with the big 'Tash first, didn't you?

And now ladies and gentlemen, sit
back and relax, don't forget to fasten your
seat belt and immerse yourself in the
riveting.

True tales of a taxi driver.

Simon Whiskey

Dogs.

We Brits love our dogs. More than we love people half the time and it's borne out by the devotion and care we lavish on them, alive or dead!

ROVER.

Operator: "Tango you want Beryl at 141 Damascus Drive. They've got a small dog. Don't be cracking any jokes or 'owt coz it's the dog's last journey if you know what I mean and Beryl's a bit upset"

And so off Tango went, practising looking concerned and serious...

He arrived at the address, a nondescript mid-terraced two-up two-down. The house number daubed in Magnolia emulsion on the red brick near the front door.

He was beckoned forth by a cigarette-wielding Beryl: Small, moustachioed, overweight. Mid-50's, her greying hair in an unkempt bundle. She had one of those massive moles on her cheek that had ten thousand thick black bristles growing out of it that a Black and Decker would have trouble shifting.

The years had not been kind to Beryl. If one was to describe her mush the word ravaged would spring to mind. When she inhaled, she had the unfortunate habit of rolling her tongue around her mouth and licking her lips, which made her look like a Bulldog licking piss off a thistle.

"C'mon young 'un, come in.' she gasped "Arry can't do any lifting on account of 'is chest y'see, poor bugger can hardly breathe"

Tango stepped through a narrow hallway festooned with ornaments, brasses and photos and on into the er.."Compact" living room.

He took in the scene: Nicotine-stained woodchip from the year dot clung to the walls. A fireplace and surround that Dickens would have recognised, and a tired vinyl covered sofa in beige against the wall. In the corner an ancient TV set with the racing on and 'Arry, in his favourite armchair facing the telly...his faded jeans and a tatty vest clung to his pale bony frame. To say he was thin was an understatement. He made a cotton bud look stocky. An oxygen bottle and equipment stood nearby.

A pedestal ashtray, topped with a pyramid of dimps and fag ash stood close by the armchair and meant economy of movement for 'Arry's right hand. With a practised flick of the wrist, he deposited another worm of ash onto the overworked device. His oxygen mask was pushed up onto his forehead,

"There's Rover" said Beryl between drags of her own embassy number 1's. "He made a funny noise about 9 o'clock last night and he's not moved since, can you 'elp me take 'im to the vets?"

The driver was non-plussed. The dog was clearly dead and rigor mortis had set in. Still, he felt obliged to join in the farce and to back out now would simply not be cricket.

Rover, the aforementioned "small dog" could have passed for a pit pony and lay on the fireside rug looking up at the driver through an eye borrowed off Columbo.

The driver knelt down and shuffled his forearms under the unfortunate animal. With some difficulty he lifted the dead weight and as he did so built-up gasses erupted from the blunt end (Of the dog, not the driver) The drivers eyes watered and he tried desperately to hold his breath, as he staggered upright through a fug of dead-dog fart.

It was at this point that 'Arry decided to join in; he leaned slightly to his right until his buttock was clear, grimaced, pursed his lips and emitted a high-pitched F sharp descending from *his* blunt end followed by a

satisfied gasp (from the non-blunt end) and
what he must have thought was a cute little
smile, that drew a stare from Beryl. 'Arry
then deftly slipped his mask over his nose
and mouth.

This addition to the room's ambience
only added to the drivers haste and he
ploughed on manfully with his face turning a
lovely plum colour, carrying the very dead,
very heavy, and very stiff dog.
Puffing with exertion, he slalomed toward the
door into the hall, dislodging brasses and
knocking over ornaments as he went. 'Arry

didn't see the funny side and admonished the driver with a mask dampened "Watch what yer doin yer fuckin clumsy bugger" He was heartened by Beryl's comment of "Don't worry love they're only shite what Arry's bought me" that drew a stare from 'Arry. It had less potency than Beryl's stare as the oxygen mask took away some of its gravitas.

Sweat sprung from the pores on the driver's forehead as he shuffled into the narrow hallway, nevertheless he gamely carried on carrying the unperturbed canine

25

out of the house.

His legs quivering under the strain, and his arms like lead he slung Rover into the boot of his taxi. An uneventful journey to the vets followed, during which Rover was no trouble at all and stayed in the boot good as gold.

The driver had just got his breath back when all too soon he arrived at the vets and once again manhandled the unfortunate creature into the busy waiting room, where he sat feeling like a complete dick with a dead dog on his lap.

Eventually, an observant Vet noticed the state of the driver- not to mention the dog, or Beryl, for that matter - and relieved the grateful driver of his charge. He wondered if

the five quid Beryl had slipped him was

worth it.

LOOFAH.

It's early evening. The driver arrives at an unfamiliar address in a fairly quiet residential area, with houses/flats occupied mostly by the elderly or the infirm.

No-one is forthcoming from the driver's horn-blast.

The driver climbs out of his taxi, and jogs up the path to the front door. The front door is ajar and so he leans in and shouts.

"Hello. Taxi!"

"I need your help, please come in" a male voice from inside replies. "Second door on the right"

Feeling a little apprehensive the driver edges inside and peers around the jamb of doorway number two.

It's the bathroom, and there in a bathtub full of soap suds is the customer, holding up a loofah.

"Just do mi back will you?" he asks sweetly.

The driver's response would make a squaddie blush, as he suggests sex and travel to the customer and he hurriedly leaves the

scene.

BOILED EGG

Young fella, late teens/early twenties, wispy goatee beard straining to grow out of his weak chin as was the fashion. Trackie bottoms half way down his backside showing ample amounts of Calvin Klein grundies. and an un-ironed plain white T shirt. He hobbles out, left leg held stiffly, and pain etched across his spotty, pale, emaciated mush.

He clambers in the back with some difficulty, for some reason holding his arse up off the seat, which is some feat with a straight leg. He addresses the perplexed looking driver.

"A and E please quick as you like"

"Roger that. What've you done fella?" the driver asks with genuine concern, although it is comical as he sees the customer, through his rear-view mirror drenched in sweat, grimacing and writhing. It's almost as if he's scared to fart.

We've all been there, in that nightmarish situation where you're desperate for a shite, and a huge bubble of wind rapidly grows inside you.

Pain

Distress.

Sweat.

 Prayers.

You've absolutely no confidence whatsoever in being able to fart controllably.

Or is it just me?

Anyway, back to the story… the customer's reply.

"I've got a boil the size of an egg on mi arse and I think it's just burst. It's fuckin killin', and it fuckin stinks"

"Keep that fuckin bum-cheek off my seats young 'un" the driver exclaimed as he rammed his Octavia into first gear and shot off like Nigel Mansell on helium, burning rubber all the way to A and E.

JOAN.

Operator: Hello A1

Customer: Hiya its Joan. One of your lads has just brought me back from' t vets.

Operator: Ok Joan what's the problem?

Joan: Can you ask 'im if I've left mi dog in his car, I can't find him.

DEAD MONEY.

T'was only the new drivers second ever job.

His first had passed without incident thank god. Easy pick up from an address he knew, a five-minute drive to the town centre and a little tip to boot. It's always nice to get the first one under your belt. Easy this taxiing malarkey.

Not every punter leaves a tip and those that don't are muttered at under the breath. It's called dead money when they give you the exact fare and no tip is forthcoming.

The newbies second customer fell into the second category, and in fact he concentrated solely on the first part of the second category by shuffling off his mortal coil during the journey.

What does one do when you crane your neck and say three pound sixty, please to be met by a corpse, I mean it's not ***that*** dear?

You can't throw him out. There's no point taking him back home. You can't get another fare. You can't leave him there and carry on because sooner or later he'll start to smell.

The taxi driver manual doesn't have a section headed 'dead passengers and what to do with them.'

Tricky one for sure.

CASANOVA.

Every taxi office has a Casanova, a Don Juan, a man so gifted by god that no woman is safe if he turns his charms upon them.

Darren Day is his hero.

He revels in his lothario lifestyle, and regales the lads in the office with his tales of conquest whilst worrying the female operators constantly. Sooner or later of course his shenanigans catch up with him and irate husbands are looking for blood.

You don't mind getting a bloody nose if you are guilty as it's an occupational hazard of being a serial shagger.

A golden rule is never to shit on your own doorstep IE: never shag a colleague's missus, or a next-door neighbour.

And so, being a conscientious shagger, he never did, and in fact offered marital advice on occasion if a pissed-up driver's wife got in his taxi who was having trouble with her fella, which is like a sheep asking a wolf what he fancies for dinner.

His advice consisted of such gems as. "Well, if you swallowed maybe, he wouldn't get so pissed off" and it was this innocuous phrase that landed him in hot water.

You see this is where the problems start. He should have kept his gob shut, and not tried to be something he isn't, something he's not really cut out for, and something nobody would believe he is. IE NOT trying to shag somebody and actually trying to help. The recipient of this sound advice is a fellow driver's wife who can't keep her gob shut and blabs to all and sundry.

It's not long before his "advice" reaches the ears of her husband. He's not the sharpest tool and all he really hears is the words Bravo (serial shagger's callsign) swallow and wife in the same sentence and knowing Bravo's reputation he puts two and two together, makes 5 and that's it, he's boiling mad. A few more pints and a recreational cigarette or two, and he's ready to rock and roll.

He, like many men when tanked up, thought he was rock hard, even though he was 5'4", thin as a rake and 8 stone wet through.

Cunning as a fox, he rings Casanova for a free lift home from the pub. Its only 400 yards but the unaware Casanova naturally comes to pick him up.

Mr Skinny says nowt 'til they pull up outside his house and then the volcano erupts.

"Have you been trying to get in my Maureen's knickers you fuckin twat?"

"No!!"

"Yeah, yer fuckin 'ave, it's all round the fuckin office you've been askin' if she swallows"

"I told her to swallow now and again to keep *YOU* happy yer fuckin prick, that's all."

He might as well have said "yes, and I did too!" For all the difference his denial made.

Mr Skinny swings and because Casanova has just at that moment glanced across at him it connects with his schnozzle.

His eyes water, his blood boils, and a trickle of claret seeps from his conk.

He gets out, walks round to the passenger side and helps Mr Skinny rather unceremoniously out of the vehicle, delivers a punch of his own to Mr Skinny's schnozzle, drawing blood.

"Ahhh. Mi fuckin snitch yer twat" says Mr Skinny. Casanova follows that up with a straight left to the gob rattling two teeth. Whilst Mr Skinny's attention is elsewhere (his wrecked mush) Bravo kicks him in the bollocks for good measure.

"Oooooffff, Mi fuckin 'Nads yer twat" Mr Skinny exclaims as he begins to crumple. Mr Skinny now has the dilemma: whether to cradle his throbbing bollocks, or nurse his aching fizzog. (His bollocks win) anyway,

Bravo grabs him by his waistband and collar and literally throws him over the fence onto his dog shit covered, weed infested lawn. Mr Skinny lies groaning on the grass. His not-at-all shocked wife comes through the front door and inquires of Bravo. "What the fucks goin' on?"

"He thinks I'm trying to get in yer knickers. He wouldn't believe me when I told him I wasn't."

"Well, he should have done. I wouldn't go near you in a month of Sundays. God knows where your peckers bin, it's probably manky"

Slightly crestfallen at Maureen's character assassination of his Todger, Bravo gets back in his Octavia and clears off.

Maureen doesn't rush to her Husband's aid but rubs verbal salt into his actual wounds with a spectacular volley.

"Serves yer right yer daft twat, you'll never fuckin learn. Get yer arse inside yer bleedin' on the path"

Inside she continues with the bollocking,

which, she assumes, is just what Mr Skinny

needs right now, it's certainly making her

feel better. She would have battered him

herself if Bravo hadn't quite literally, beaten her to the punch.

The next day, full of chagrin, Mr Skinny rings and apologises to Bravo, blaming the booze and skank for his behaviour, promising never to do it again.

A JOUSTER.

The vast majority of daytime jobs are
ferrying old folk to the supermarket and back
or, down to the town centre so they can call
in the indoor market. They take an age to
come out of the house, and then go back in
because they've forgotten their stick. Then
they turn back to check the front door,
swinging on the handle like a demon. Then
they check their handbag for their keys before
eventually clambering in. They like to get in
the front because there's more room than in

the back. Then it's a wrestling bout with the seat belt which the seat belt usually wins by submission. For some reason they can't get the buckle in the slot and all drivers are adept at putting a passenger's seat belt in for them left-handed whilst driving.

Some prefer the back though…………….

Most elderly people usually make a dog's dinner of getting in, or, out of a taxi. A contributing factor is they insist on keeping hold of their walking sticks.

When one is young and supple, the operation is without hindrance, a doddle, but as the year's advance something seems to happen and it becomes like the Krypton Factor assault course.

In this particular case as the visually impaired, unsteady on her legs grey haired bent elderly lady made her way to the taxi, she unknowingly dipped the toe of her walking stick into a soft, fresh, pile of dog shit.

Some old dears throw their sticks onto the back seat like a javelin, and then clamber in after them. Some keep hold of them and perform a comedy routine like the billiard scene in the Pink Panther as they interfere with the manoeuvre when trying to get in.

This dear old lady however had her own technique. She held it out in front of her, much akin to a jouster with his lance.

Her target on this occasion though was neither the upholstery, nor the window. Instead, she poked it unceremoniously into the dozing drivers' ear'ole, thereby depositing a blob of dog shite into his shell like.

He could smell shite throughout the mercifully short journey to the shops, and presumed that the old dear had shat herself, or, unknowingly trod in a dog turd just before getting in.

He wasn't looking forward to cleaning it up. When she got out, he inspected the rear carpet but found nothing, but the smell was, if anything worse. Driving back to base he kept looking over his left shoulder as that's where the stench was coming from.

Back at base he asked another driver if *he* could smell dog shit.

"Not only can I smell it" he replied "I can see it"

"See it! What do you mean, see it?"

"It's in yer 'earole. yer dirty bastard"

"WHAT!"

The driver checks in the mirror, remembers the old dear poking him in the ear and swiftly drives home to shower.

Is that why Van Gogh did what he did, he wonders?

WASTE OF TIME.

Trips to and from the hospital are a staple diet of the cabbie.

Listening in rapt attention as ailments are described in excruciating detail. Gammy legs are the most prevalent, especially amongst the elderly.

A pick up from the mental health ward is rare, for obvious reasons. But occasionally they do happen. One assumes a visitor is the customer because inmates are usually easy to spot. However...

Well dressed, (not in pyjamas and dressing gown) gentleman waiting outside the portico, a Visitors lanyard around his neck. Shoes on, (not slippers which is a big giveaway) hair combed and general air of respectability. He climbs in.

"Where to Guv?"

"Gee cross please driver I'll direct you from there."

Nice, thinks the driver a tenner easy.

An uneventful 15 minutes later and Gee cross is in sight.

"Just pull up at the little Tesco's first please"

Even better thinks the driver, he likes the "first" bit. 10 minutes pass and the customer eventually reappeared without any discernible purchases, meters showing £14 and counting.

"I've got to drop by my sisters for a sec, the customer adds, "Montague Road please."

"In Ashton?" says the cabbie hopefully

"That's the one"

Woo hoo! thinks the driver, that's near the hospital where they've just come from that's another £10 in the bag. They arrive and the customer leaps out with a "won't be a tick" and disappears round the back. The driver gets a tad concerned as time marches on but 15 minutes later he's back.

"Train station now fella" he pipes.

"Ashton?" inquires the driver

"No Piccadilly"

The driver can barely contain himself. Another £15 at least, the meters on £25 already lucky day or what!

They're half way to Piccadilly when the radio crackles to life.

"Oscar"

"You rang"

"Have you picked up at the hospital?"

"Sure, have almost an hour ago"

"Well take him back will you he's escaped."

"WHAT! What do you mean, He's escaped?"

"He's an inmate. They've been looking for him for over an hour."

"But, but, the fuckin meter's showing £35.50"

Considerate as ever, the operator softens the blow.

"Tough titty".

CAMPING.

When one climbs into one's taxi to start a shift, the thought that one might be attacked depends on the customers (and their numbers) time (whether they're pissed) and the area.

3:30 pm on a Saturday afternoon, and a smartly dressed middle aged husband and wife is about as safe as it can get.

Except that she's had a sherry or two, and is, a little bit uppity. Her frock is 1980's Joan Collins straight out of Dynasty, the shoulder pads borrowed from a line-backer, and hair and make-up by Liberace. There could be a mouse or a gerbil in there easy.

Her husband (who looks nothing like Blake Carrington) is er.., relaxed shall we say and is quickly on his I-phone.

For some reason Joan Collins takes a dislike to the driver/and or his driving/and or his route/and or the fact that he's breathing without her permission and because her attentive husband is ignoring her with the aplomb only long-suffering marrieds can, she starts an argument with the driver about the first thing that comes into her head. The driver doesn't respond in the correct manner or with the correct words and so she leans forward, wraps her arms around his neck and proceeds to choke him. She's squeezing with all her might.

Taken off guard the driver (eyes bulging and face a nice purple colour) looks imploringly at the husband through the rear-view mirror. The grunting noises must have disturbed him because he glances up; takes in the attempted murder of the driver of the taxi he's in and mouths "Candy Crush" whilst motioning to his i-phone to the bloodshot eyes he can see reflected in the mirror.

'Fair do's' thinks the driver, and realizing he'll have to extricate himself, reaches into the door pocket for his trusty friend, a small rubber mallet he keeps for just such an occasion, either that, or, if he has a sudden desire to pitch a tent and needs to bang in his tent pegs.

He doesn't fancy burning sausages and singing Row, row, row your boat, around a campfire at the mo, so instead, swinging over his left shoulder he wallops the woman square in the forehead.

It has the desired effect and her grip loosens, as it usually does when you're unconscious. She slumps back; the driver quickly pulls up, drags Joan Collins unceremoniously out of the taxi, dumps her on the pavement and jumps back in ready to hare off tout suite. You've guessed it dear reader; still engrossed in a nightmarishly hard level in the back seat is her loving husband.

"Oi…. Numb nuts" says the driver.

The husband looks up "What's up?" he belches at the driver.

"Fuck off," said the driver.

So, he did.

DEMON DRINK.

Some punters like a drink. Now't wrong with that, indeed punters who like a drink account for a good many fares.

Some punters take it a bit too far though. Havin' Guinness on your cornies is a tad over the top in my book but there y'go.

They usually live alone because their alcoholism has wrecked any relationship they may have had, so they have no-one to act as their conscience, or as a guiding hand on the tiller. They live on benefits because they're unemployable. Even though they can still semi-function because they're so used to it, they are still permanently three parts pissed. Indeed, one Alki (alcoholic) told me that he had to take a six pack up to bed because he HAD to crack one open as soon as he woke up, before he'd even scratched his balls and farted.

You get to know the stay-at-home-coz-they-can't-be-arsed getting dressed/washed and it's loads cheaper to buy from off licence alkies very well, as they use taxis on a daily basis and many times more than once a day.

They've been alkies for years and know every driver well enough to trust them to go shopping for the booze.

A rarity is a couple who are *both* alkies, in which case it's a match made in heaven for them and a nightmare for the cabbie, knowing when you get the job it's more of a 'big shop' than just a booze run.

You arrive and collect the money and take their order: Six 3 litre bottles of white lightning, (the stuff is so potent it'd strip the paint off the Forth Bridge), three 1 litre bottles of 'My mums' Vodka, which is about

71

3 pence a litre which tells you all you need to know about its quality, and 4 packets of Silk Cut. As you're leaving, he shouts to her "Do you want him to get anything for dinner love?"

"Yeah, I'll have a Mars bar" she replies as she twists the cap off their breakfast.

The driver makes his way to the 'Offy and pays at the till looking to all the world like a raging alcoholic taxi driver It's back to the ranch and as usual there's no tip and not so much as a 'kiss mi arse' from the duo.

A quick point about alkies that the normal man in the street may not realise is that Alkies don't drink every bit of booze they can lay their hands on, as you would imagine, oh no. They stick to one poison and get so used to it that they can still function even when you or I would be dead. An Alki who drinks only Vodka say, can drink four bottles a day and it's like pop, but would be unconscious after 5 pints of Stella.

Some punters who maybe use a taxi once every blue moon aren't really tuned in as to how things work.......

Operator: Hello A1

Customer: Hello I'd like to book a taxi to the airport please.

Operator: OK love when for?

Customer: 6 AM Monday morning.

Operator: Lovely, where are you off to?

Customer: 2 weeks in the Algarve.

Operator: OK love what's your address?

Customer: (indignantly) I'm not giving you that! I've just told you I'm leaving the country, any Tom, Dick or Harry could

burgle me at their leisure!

Operator: Apart from the fact we don't

have a Tom or Harry but plenty of Dicks,

how are we going to pick you up?

Customer: (Pause) Well………. (Pause)

I know!…..you can pick me up from next

door!

CAULIFLOWER.

It's two years later and the same driver gets called to the same address,

Perhaps the occupant is different this time though, but still, he girdles his loins.

The door is ajar again!

"Hello! Taxi!" he shouts and there's a definite tremor in his voice. "You're not in't bath, are you?

"Of course not! Don't be silly, I'm in the front room"

Is it the same voice? He can't be sure.

There was definitely something different about it, but he couldn't quite say what it was. Gripped by indecision, he doesn't want to appear foolish in front of what could be an innocent chap who just needs help getting out of his chair, or, putting his shoes on.

He follows the sound of the voice and peers round the doorway.

The customer's not in the bath it's true, for one very good reason. It's not the bathroom. He could have been though because he's stark bollock naked! He's perched on a dining chair molesting a

Cauliflower in a rather loving fashion whilst pulling it onto his coitus erectus, hence the strange voice as he's in some sort of throe.

Not surprisingly the driver didn't hang around to hear his request this time, and took a dim view of the job, beat a hasty retreat and went home for a very stiff drink. The long-lasting effect was the driver's future revulsion to his wife's home-made cauliflower cheese.

OPERATOR.

Dear reader, one might think the job of the operator is mundane, lacking in excitement, or, danger, and one would be right, most of the time, if not almost *all* of the time. The weekend drunks not- withstanding, with their verbal abuse which operators shrug off a 'la a Ducks back.

However, one day said operator, dozing serenely in his hutch whilst fielding the odd call from Joe public, and trying to beat his best score on Candy Crush, gets run over.

That's right reader, RTA as the boys in blue call it. Road traffic accident. How is that possible? To get mown down whilst sat at your desk removing ear wax with the end of a pen. Here's how.

Dear old lady 80'S (again) on her way for her Thursday perm before a Caribbean cruise sailing on the Sunday.

She's in a courtesy car as her 1990 fiesta is in dock and for some un-known reason, they plonk her in an automatic Peugeot 3008 SUV. It's only got two pedals instead of three so that should help surely. She's not called

Shirley she's called Doreen by the way.
Anyway, instead of helping it serves to
confuse.

There's a good 20 feet between the
parking bay and the front of the timber and
glass office/hutch which the operator dozes
in.

A kerb is thrown in by the council for
good measure but this proves to be no
obstacle whatsoever as she (god knows how)
turns into the parking bay, fails to stop,
bounces up the kerb, accelerates again and
smashes into the front of the office, writing

off the SUV, the office, and breaking the ribs and wrist of said operator.

Fire engine, ambulance, police, all attend, and like the crowd that gathered all scratch their heads as to how she managed it.

I really hope the operator had the wit (when he came to) to ask "where to love?" but I doubt it

To top it all, would you believe ladies and gentlemen she still made her appointment, a tad late but, that's understandable considering she'd just caused £75,000.00 worth of damage to somebody

else's office, written off a car that wasn't

hers, and nearly killed a bloke.

Nothing comes between a woman and

her hair appointment as any man will testify.

WHY IS BIZ BROWN?

Young mum 18 or 19, Sporty Spice wannabe, climbs in with 3- or 4-year-old little lad called Keegan (whatever) It looks like Keegan's applied his mum's make up this morning using his plastic Bob the builder trowel.

He's a cheeky chappie you can tell, and his mum, stinking of weed and clutching her i-phone as if her life depended on it has just overdosed on Peter Kay.

"'Ave yer bin busy" she chirrups soon

as the door is slammed shut.

Without pausing for breath it's, "is this your own car", swiftly followed by "what time yer on 'til"

Good grief thinks the driver, is she going for some kind of record.

Keegan then joins in, and why not, why should his mum have all the fun?

"Can I ask a question of the mister man mummy?"

"No, you can't" says mum "stop pestering him, he's driving"

"Aw please mummy, just one"

85

"Alright then" sporty shouts, with a hint of petulance.

"Goody" says Keegan

"Mister, why is biz brown?"

LOST PROPERTY.

The contents of the lost property box, as you can probably guess dear reader, is a fairly straight forward affair, apart from Joan of course who loses dogs and Sunday dinners.

Keys, phones, umbrellas, wallets, purses, lighters, fags, johnnies, bank cards, lippy, jewellery, knickers, shoe(s), (how can you not notice one shoe missing??!!) hats, gloves, scarves, teddies, fidget spinners, hearing aids, walking sticks, false teeth!!!!(how drunk do you have to be to not notice THAT!!!!)

The first prize though must go to the driver who brought in a buggy. Full sized mind you, not a kid's toy, and also containing a toddler, also full sized. A funny item, I'm sure you agree, sadly the reason behind it is more sobering.

The child's Mother, in fear for her life and that of her offspring at the hands of an abusive, violent man, took the extraordinary step of leaving the toddler in the pushchair in the cab, and pleading with the driver to look after the child, knowing a beating awaited her at home, and possible harm may come to her baby. The body shudders at the state of mind of that poor woman, who had to leave her baby with a stranger to secure its safety.

HAPPY BIRTHDAY!

There's now't as queer as folk, as the northern saying goes. It's true n'all.

Operator: Hello A1

Customer: Hiya can you send a car round for now.

Operator: Where are you love?

Customer: 35 Lord Street.

Operator: What's yer name and where you going?

Customer: Britney, and Er… well, nowhere really.

Operator: Oh.

Customer: I just want the driver to drive around for 20 minutes or so.

Operator: Er, right, (no human being could leave it at that, and quite rightly the operator had to ask)

Why?

Customer: Well, it's my boyfriend's birthday, and I didn't know what to get him, so, I'm going to suck him off in the back of the taxi whilst the driver just drives around.

Operator: Right then, I'll er…send him round!!!!!!!

What's wrong with some underpants and a lynx gift set? The mind boggles as to her plans for the lucky fella's 40[th.]

DOUGIE.

It's not always a bed of roses y'know, this taxiing lark.

Some customers have a tendency to smell. Indeed, some are truly ripe and the fumes coming off them defy description, but the worst?

Meet Dougie. If he was a cartoon there'd be half a dozen flies constantly buzzing above his head. Unfortunately, he wasn't a cartoon, and any real-life self-respecting fly would think twice about landing on Dougie's noggin.

You'd rather be on the deck of a trawler off the Dogger Bank in mid-winter, wearing only your Y fronts and wellies than pick him up.

This would be the third time this driver had picked him up in about nine months. He was distraught, and almost crying as Dougie shuffled over. Pot-bellied, unkempt, slovenly.

Once again, he was wearing the same faded black Iron Maiden T shirt and faded black joggers as he had the previous two times the unfortunate driver had fallen foul of

the private hire gods. The ensemble hadn't

seen the inside of a washing machine in the

intervening months, nor his skin been

introduced to a bar of imperial leather.

Dougie's long, greying, unkempt thinning

hair, hadn't felt a drop of Vosene either. He

also had two of those funny thingies stuck on

his scalp that look like soggy cornflakes. His

feet, clad in the same desert wellies no matter

what the season, sported toenails an Orc

would admire. A "dusting" of dandruff on the

shoulders of his T shirt looked like the top of

a Victoria sponge; the stains and leftovers still attached to his top would have made a three-course meal for some starving bugger somewhere.

The stains on his joggers remain un-mentionable. He wasn't what you'd call a 'catch' unless you wanted to catch something you'd rather not.

Dougie's aversion to washing his clothes (one dreads to think about his undergarments) naturally applied to the skin he was surrounded in. He didn't trouble the plumbing in his tax-payer funded flat, except for the WC of course. Boy did he pong! Old armpit sweat, unwashed feet, that funny groiny smell. Make a charging Rhino's eyes water at 30 paces easy.

He also possessed a slack arse. He seemed to pride himself on the quantity and quality of his farts, and often congratulated himself after he had dropped his guts moments after getting in.

Dougie himself was no George Clooney. An unfortunate ailment (the refusal to wash) meant dry, flaky, blotchy skin, coupled with extremely greasy hair and nicotine-stained

fingers and nails the colour of mahogany,
they looked like they belonged to some
geezer that's just been dug up after 10,000
years in a peat bog, or, been discovered
poking out of the permafrost halfway up a
glacier in Starsgordvarkland.

There was a dark grey/black finish to the
underside of his quite long nails which
completed his look. Not forgetting his breath
(how could we), Jesus. 10 million fags a
week. A redundant toothbrush. He had the
breath of a thousand goats. His sparse teeth

were rarely seen (a blessing) as they hid behind a straggly grey/nicotine tinted 'tash.

If all that wasn't enough, Dougie liked to cough regularly. Sometimes a dry hacking cough, sometimes more of a "let's see how much phlegm and catarrh I can retrieve from the back of my throat and lungs to chew momentarily and re-swallow" kind of cough. He never troubled himself with the decency to cover his mouth.

He <u>always</u> sat in the front!!!!

Because his carer?!(Who patently *didn't* care sat in the back!)

The driver's window was fully down no matter what the weather, and if holding one's breath was an Olympic event then the pearl divers of Sarawak would have to content themselves with silver.

HEFTY TIP.

Tips, we all like 'em.

Especially hefty ones, though they are infrequent.

More frequent are titchy ones, especially from elderly folk who have lived through the war. Boy, do they know hardship and the value of things.

They often make a production of giving a tip. Making you fish around in your bum bag for ages finding ten pence change, then giving you a *different* ten pence piece as a fuckin tip! Oft accompanied with the words "buy yourself a coffee young man"

Buy yerself a coffee with a10 pence!!

Are you havin' a Turkish?

When was the last time you bought a coffee for Christ's sake? A coffee *bean* more like.

We've heard them all too. Punters like to make a joke and laugh there balls off when they crack a tip gag, we've heard a million times before. Don't eat yellow snow. Don't count your money over a grid. Dusty carpet in the 3:15 at Haydock.

Occasionally, very occasionally, a tip is forthcoming which restores one's faith in human nature.

One such involved a dear old lady (yet again! You're getting the picture now aren't you) closer to 100 years old than 70 on a yearly trip to the Spanish consulate in Manchester. A £15 fare tops.

"You'll come back for me won't you young man (methuselah was young compared to her) when I ring in about an hour. I'll pay you now though if that's alright" and handed over a sealed envelope. A bulging one at that!

The driver tootles round the corner after dropping her off and rips open the envelope, breaking a nail in the process.

It's worth it as there's £200.00 inside. A £185.00 tip!

What a lovely old lady! I wonder if she needs a new driveway or her curtains cleaning?

He's tempted to ring her every week posing as Pedro Gonzales from the consulate asking her to come in and try the Paella.

DIM BULBS.

Let me make one thing crystal clear before this next story is told. Taxi drivers perform a fantastic service to the transport departments of local authorities. Ferrying special needs/autistic children to and from schools every day and getting to know those children and forming a bond with them. Of course, we get paid for it but it is still a massive help to the children's parents/Carers and the system as a whole.

Not all the kids that get a free lift to school are special needs or Autistic. Sometimes they are just disruptive/aggressive/un-manageable in Mainstream schools and slip down the ladder 'til they reach the bottom rung and end up at schools for naughty boys and girls, where it's basically somewhere for them to go between 9 and 3. They've missed out on a lot of their education because of their behaviour and are therefore, er, how can I put it politely? un-educated. They're pretty dim bulbs. In some cases, they have to have an escort with them to assist the driver, so he can concentrate on driving and the escort tries to keep the passenger occupied. (On one occasion when the escort was off, the little cherub threw a full litre bottle of milk out the passenger window, narrowly missing an oncoming Jag.) That gives you some idea of what they're capable of if left unattended.

However, on this occasion to pass the time after months of mind-numbing boredom the escort suggested a game of Hangman with the little cherub.

He readily agreed.

The escort (a lovely woman) wrote down   -/-/-

A three-letter word which one would have hoped wouldn't be too taxing.

After Ten minutes the little lad had reached this point D/-/G.

She prompted him, she cajoled and coaxed and encouraged him and eventually his little 10-year-old index finger shot up!

"Doughnut" he cried, beaming from ear to ear.

Jesus fuckin Christ!

After a period of recovery, and some months later and with a different kid, I-Spy was suggested.

Just in the environs of the car was the rule, nothing outside.

"I spy with my likkle eye something beginning with "C" the dim bulb said.

Now there's not a lot of "C's" in a car and so 5 minutes later guesses are very thin, and so eventually the escort and driver admit defeat and say "Give up, what is it?"

"Corner" says the dimmest of bulbs pointing to the join between dashboard and door.

FFS.

Eyes were rolled, fists were clenched, and groans emitted, and it was decided there and then *never* to play any more games!

A bit more Joan

Operator: Hello A1

Customer: Hiya its Joan.

Operator: Go on Joan.

Joan: Well, I've just come 'ome in a black cab, can't remember which one, but can you ask 'em to check if anyone of 'em's found mi Sunday dinner?

Sometimes experiences come out of the blue, and when you least expect them, and boy do they live long in the memory as this next story shows.

TRIXIE.

May Bank holiday Monday. Normally fairly quiet as local folk queue to get to Blackpool.

The odd middle-aged couple go out for a swift half at the con club.

A standard 1950's semi on a much-frequented Dukinfield estate would change all that for one driver as he picks up the nondescript 35-year-old at 2pm. He still lives with his dad so that tells you something about the geezer. He's so ordinary you'd forget him in a heartbeat after an introduction.

He's had a Shandy or two and is already three-parts pissed.

The first port of call is the cash machine. He's as trusting as a new-born so he passes the driver his bank card and asks him to get the dosh out for him because he's a bit wobbly. £200.00. He directs the driver to Tib Street in town. The driver's pleased as this is a good fare, and if he was walking, he would have a spring in his step. But he's not, so he doesn't.

At Tib Street the customer asks the driver to wait and he disappears inside a sex shop. Five minutes later he returns clutching a carrier bag and directs the driver to the Red-Light District.

The driver squirms in his seat but the meter's running so he gamely carries on.

Down a squalid back street, a working girl is spotted, and the driver is asked to sidle up.

The lady is on the plump-ish side but not too bad, too heavily made up as one would expect, and of course scantily clad.

As they near her she puffs on a cigarette and squints sexily (though that might be cigarette smoke going in her eyes) and gives them her best "come hither" look.

Her allure is punctured when she opens her gob and treats the pair to a gummy smile, interrupted only by one yellowed and stained tusk protruding from her upper gum like a single wet sock on a washing line.

Un-originally, she asks, "You looking for business?"

Dentistry is the first thought in the driver's mind. What a good business. The customer isn't too choosy and he invites her into the taxi. She clambers in and it's off back to Dukinfield.

The customer proudly shows his purchase to his new best friend- a maid's outfit!

"It's too small for me, I'll never get into that" she exclaimed. It was true; she had shoehorned herself into her work clothes and they bulged in all the wrong places. She looked like two pound of sausages in a one-pound bag, or a burst sofa, take your pick. The driver, hoping to assist (nosey as ever) turns to have a look and notices a distinct lack of undergarments on the latest recruit.

"Tha's got no trollies on!" he remarks.

"I find they only get in the way dearie"
she answers without a trace of irony.

They return to the starting point and the
quick-thinking driver gives Trixie (they've
made introductions on the journey) his
mobile number ready for the return journey-
which he feels won't be too long in coming.
(Couldn't resist that one)

One can only guess at the shenanigans
that went on inside, but the driver doubts they
were re-enacting a love scene from Dr
Zhivago.

Sure enough Twenty minutes later his phone rings and as he's luckily round the corner they're soon on the way back to Trixie's home patch.

Caringly the driver asks "How did it go?"

"Easiest ton I've ever made. Bit of a dance and he shot his load soon as I got mi tits out."

In fact, it would later come to light that on the way back down stairs after her performance she spotted the man's father dozing in an armchair. He must have been a light sleeper as there was a bulge in the front of his trousers, and when he "awoke" Trixie was riding him like Lester Piggott.

Unfortunately, "Daddy" was no Nijinsky and when she sauntered out just

Five minutes later his bulge had already receded. As he slumped in his armchair, happy and sated, he noticed the lack of another bulge that he used to have in the back of his trousers.

Whilst in a post coital daze she'd relieved him of his wallet!

One has to admire her quickness of thought. Fagin would have been doing a jig.

ASSAULT.

Sometimes dear reader the laughs stop, and real terror takes over.

Many drivers I have known have been assaulted, or, stabbed or both.

One such occasion I shall describe to you whilst you get your breath back from all the side splittingly funny tales you've just read.

5AM. Winter. Dark. Quiet. Well known rough estate but an unfamiliar address.

Two men waiting outside; early morning

workers perhaps whose car is in dock. The driver (late 50's overweight, no threat to anyone or anything except the kebab shop) is watchful but sees, nor senses any evidence of the impending violence.

They're waiting on the wrong side of the street so he moves across the road to pull up beside them. A mistake.

Without warning and with surprising ferocity, one of them swiftly opens the driver's door and starts yanking him out of the car, he's old school so he doesn't wear a seatbelt and as he's dragged from his car, he's smashed in the mouth with a rounders bat. Blood and teeth erupt from the drivers wrecked mouth, and another blow is administered to his head which leaves him semi-conscious.

He's dumped on the pavement and his attackers ransack his money bag and rifle his pockets, taking his phone. His watch is ripped from his wrist and he's given a kick in the gonads for good measure before the attackers jump in his car and drive away……………

The whole assault is over in seconds. Eventually, blood still pouring from his mouth and head, he managed to stumble to a nearby house and wake the occupants.

His car was found some miles away in a right state and no-one has been apprehended for the crime.

He's back behind the wheel four days later. There's no sick pay and food has to be put on the table, and bills need to be paid

POLLY.

Three girls all under 10 years old pile in the back and immediately there's a scrum because no-one wants to sit in the middle. Eldest girl baggsies a window seat so the one forced in the middle throws the biggest tantrum ever. The screaming is ear splitting. Mum chips in with the classic line "Stop fuckin' startin'" They don't stop starting so Mum shouts "Savannah, swap with Candice or were not fuckin goin'". Peace is restored but glares are exchanged and one can sense a growing unease in the back. Mum gets in the front, (a regular known as "Bizteeth" would you believe? presumably because she never brushes them) more tattoos than Amy Housewine, hair scraped up in a bun so tight it pulls her pants up, off white Reebok trainers, black McKenzie trackies, grey Henley's vest top, Paul's Couture oversized handbag, earrings the size of bicycle tyres, more necklaces than Mr T and make-up by Stevie Wonder. I wouldn't like to say she was rough, but she made a bear's arse look smooth and attractive.

On her knee a shoebox, liberally sprinkled with holes the diameter of a pencil.

"Goolies" she says.

The destination is *Gourleys* vets. She's not the first and it's an old joke so the driver knows it's not an exclamation, statement or insult but an instruction and he knows where he's going.

Is it a hamster? A mouse, or gerbil, or Guinea pig even. God forbid a rat, or a Ferret. He cannot resist the temptation and has to ask a la Brad Pitt in Se7en "What's in the box"?

With a flourish straight from the lovely Debbie McGhee's repertoire she whips off the shoe box lid to reveal a Budgie. A blue one, (Not the only similarity it has with a Parrot of the Norwegian blue variety.) nestling serenely on a bed of bog roll.

"She's called Polly" Bizteeth declares, as if that's an unusual name for a Budgie whilst treating the driver to a smile which he wished she hadn't bothered with as it was a trifle off-putting.

One would expect Polly to jump up after being contained in such a fashion, shit for

England and then fly off to resume the rest of her life, but no, not a flicker, not a movement of an eye that looks suspiciously glassy, or the test of a wing, mainly because there was an elastic band round the poor bugger.

"Polly fell off her perch this morning, so we put her on the kitchen table but Chantelle-Rae swears she saw her move when she was havin' her coco pops, so we thought we'd better get her checked out y'know. The lacky bands so she dun't fuck off when we take the lid off, int that right girls?" A chorus of "yeah's" from the back seat and Chantelle Rae beams that she got a mention.

"She only moved coz Channy flicked her" says the girl in the middle, who isn't beaming and therefore isn't Chantelle Rae.

"No, I fuckin never" retorts Channy.

"Yeah, yer fuckin did I fuckin saw yer"

"Fuckin dint" Channy mutters but looks downcast.

"Did yer Channy?" Inquiries Bizteeth, turning around to look at her, giving the driver a good waft of Anais Anais, stale fag breath, and B.O. as she does so.

"Yer better fuckin not 'ave coz it's costing me a fuckin bomb this taxi"

There goes mi tip thinks the driver. Thankfully Channy doesn't respond again and just looks out of the window sulkily, consoling herself by picking her nose and eating the fruits of her excavations. The journey is mercifully short and the driver is glad to be rid of the Clampits.

HOLOGRAM.

You think you've heard it all after taxiing for ages, but every now and again, one sneaks up on you when you're least expecting it. When the unknown customer is

a respectable middle-aged

lady…………..

Some people form friendships in nursery, and they carry on throughout life and become things of beauty. Women in particular are able to tell their special, closest friends all their intimate details and things no other human on the planet knows about.

Until they get in a cab of course and for some reason decide that the cabbie is really a hologram and not a human being and therefore they can become a confidante whether they like it or not.

One such woman, Mid-50's perhaps, nothing remarkable about her appearance, or, demeanour, the driver had never seen her before.

She's off to the hospital so won't drive coz parking's a nightmare!

So, a cab ride is a bit of an adventure after years of driving herself, and even the impending appointment can't dampen her sprits.

The usual questions are soon exhausted and then she inquires "How'd you go on y'know, when the office was shut, coz it was wrecked you know, needing the toilet"

A fair question I suppose and pleasing because it's off Piste.

"Well, there's Morrison's or Asda or Tesco's or you could always go home if you're near it" the driver replies.

The driver at this point thinks this is a boring, far too factual answer and decides to lighten the mood with a jocular addition.

Not to be taken literally.

He didn't mean it.

He was kidding.

He'd made it up.

He wasn't being serious.

Easily noticeable by the laugh and funny pulled face.

"Or of course you can just shit in your pants ha ha."

Customer: "Well I did that the other day"

WTF!

"I went to the loo and when I got up, I realized I hadn't pulled mi knickers down, right mess I was I can tell you"

Jesus fuckin Christ woman! I don't know you! We've never met before. Why are you telling me this? Please stop! I can't get the image out of my head and you're sat right next to me and smiling like it's a normal convo. Please, shut the fuck up I'm embarrassed for you!

"Had a lot of weather lately 'ant we?"

Said the driver hastily, changing the

topic.

DESPERADO!

Sometimes ladies and gentlemen the fact that as a taxi driver you can be on the road for a considerable period of time, means that toilet breaks are a constant thorn in your, er, side. Especially if you've mistakenly had a curry and a couple of sherry's the night before and a number two is brewing.

Now imagine its Sunday morning 9:30. You're picking up at the airport where you cannot just whip to the loo because the traffic marshals (who make the gestapo look like lollipop men) won't allow it (you'll be fined and tortured and your vehicle will be crushed). You think you'll be ok until the customers come out and you realise there's three drop offs. The last being miles away from anywhere in some posh village where public bogs are unheard of.

Tango drives like Nigel Mansell on helium as the bubbles grow and grow. Each drop off takes an age as a thousand goodbyes and kisses and see-you-soons are exchanged.

The driver is in a severe state of distress and is even contemplating asking the last customer if he can take a shit at her house.

She's as posh as they come and her house and gardens are the size of Hampshire, so he chickens out preferring if need be, to heavily soil himself once off the gravelled drive.

He experiences a slight respite but previous episodes have taught him it will be short lived and that soon the menace will return.

He desperately searches for an open pub or supermarket but its Sunday morning in the middle of fuckin nowhere. He's re-inventing the definition of desperate.

At last, he sees a boozer at a junction and he turns into the car park-cum-beer garden area at the back.

He gingerly manages somehow to get out of the taxi whilst not shitting himself. He's pouring in sweat and his face is a contortion of agony as a huge bubble builds within his back passage.

He can wait no longer and swallowing his pride he dives behind a carling black label advertising wind break that is near the back door of the (thankfully closed) pub.

He hastily drops his Trackie bottoms and grundies, pushes his todger down so he doesn't piss all over his clobber, holds onto the windbreak and squats as an immediate torrent of squit like lava pours out of him for what seems like an age. By the time he's finished his face is like a plum and his bum hole like a blood orange.

Breathless and pouring in sweat he rests for a minute, gathering his strength for he knows his ordeal is not yet over. He prays to all the gods that the landlord doesn't choose this moment to sneak out for a crafty fag.

Soon, his muscles clench again and this time he's sure he's parting with a huge lump of coal. Unable to breathe because the thrutching is so intense and lengthy he goes a bit dizzy and almost faints. Luckily, the revolting stench of the manure he's just deposited acts like sniffing salts and brings him back to his senses. It's so bad it'd make a

maggot gag.

The relief though!!!! Oh my god!!!!

He takes a minute to recover, panting

and sweating, until eventually his thoughts

return to the immediate situation.

He doesn't want to get back in his taxi

with his hairy, spotty, arsehole all shitty.

Obviously, there's no bog roll so this presents

a problem. There is really only one option.

His grundies will have to deputise as bog roll.

Now he has to somehow remove them

with the use of only one hand, whilst

continuing to squat out of sight behind a windbreak. His thighs burned, and new sweat sprung from his already overworked pores as he balanced on one leg removing trainers, trackie bottoms, and underpants, whilst not dipping them into the still warm pile of shite just inches from his bollocks. A quick wipe and it was job done. Houdini would have been proud.

As he swiftly climbed into his car and roared away, he did spare a thought for the landlord who, when setting up for the day would find a steaming pyramid of shite with

a Y front topping outside his back door.

UTTER RUBBISH.

Talking Bollocks! It's what punters do best and boy oh boy do they like it.

The poor cabbie has to sit and listen to some absolute crap believe me. Here's an example, I'll set the scene.

King Street is a typical northern B-Road through a typical northern town. Rows of terraced houses and double yellow lines all over the place because it's a bus route. Residents can't park right outside their house but naturally they occasionally park up half on half off the pavement whilst they unload shopping or get the young 'un's out.

One such occasion caused the luckless cabbie to stop whilst oncoming traffic came past. Cue verbal diarrhoea from thick punter. "What the fuck is that prat doin? It's a main road the fuckin dick. They shouldn't allow people to have cars if they buy a house on this street!"

The scary thing is he (Only a man could say something so stupid but think it right) believed it. The righteous indignation on his bovine mush confirmed he wasn't joking.

God help us!

So according to the half-wit you're not *allowed* to buy a house on King Street if you own a car. What a prat!

You do see *some* extraordinary things when you are driving about. Once in a lifetime thing that are admittedly of no importance whatsoever, but are nice little anecdotes.

Now then here's one for you.

When was the last time you saw a three-legged dog? Even if it was yesterday, when was the last time you saw one BEFORE that? And the one BEFORE that!!! Well dear reader, believe it or not the record is 3 *different* three-legged dogs on three *consecutive* days. Beat that!

RHOTACISM.

Some folk have the above condition. It's where you have difficulty pronouncing the letter 'R'.

Firstly, which arsehole called it Rhotacism, which obviously begins with an 'R'. Probably the same arsehole that decided bad breath should be called Halitosis!

Anyway, loads of people go through life with it and it never causes a problem. It even helps some as a kind of trademark (think Jonathan Ross).

Even being a radio operator at a taxi firm where the word Roger is used all the time is not inhibitive.

However, there's always one occasion when things transpire to produce a comic occurrence which even the operator chuckled at.

The operators Rhotacism wasn't very pronounced and was a sort of mixing of the letters R and W, reminiscent of the actor Terry Thomas saying the word wready.

Everybody was used to it and never gave it a second thought.

It's a busy Friday night and Roger whose call sign is Rio blows on the middle plot.

Operator: "Wodger Wio yer one", which sounds like it begins with a 'W' when it doesn't.

Moments later:

Operator: "Wio, y'want Woberts at the Wed lion, he's in the wight hand woom and he's weaving a wed jacket."

Where's Joan when you need her at Asda.

PSYCHO.

After a while you get a sort of "nose" for the customer who is a psycho.

There's usually some "tell" or giveaway that this someone is not quite right, that the wires are loose.

They're usually harmless if not antagonised, and best ignored, with the occasional grunt of agreement when a question which you've not understood or heard properly is asked. However, occasionally one slips through the net…..

8:30am Sunny Tuesday morning in June, a school day.

Unsuspecting driver picks up man and woman, anywhere between 25 and 40, both scruffy in a studenty kind of way but obviously not students. They both smell like a damp cellar. They've both had a drink and a recreational cigarette or two and it transpires they've been boozing and smoking pot all night.

She's trying to calm him down but he's insistent they go to Mossley to visit his sister whose had some trouble with her boyfriend, and also collect some money he's owed off some geezer called Jonno.

He offers the driver £20 straight away to cover the fare because they might want to come straight back. The grateful driver trousers the dosh and his initial misgivings are allayed.

Not for long.

On the 15-minute journey up there the chap mutters constantly under his breath. The driver only catches snippets. Like, "I'll rip the cunts neck out"

"Oh dear" thinks the driver. Thanking all the gods he's already got some bugs bunny.

They arrive at the destination, a council estate of dubious reputation; garden gates and fences are a luxury, and lawnmowers a thing of the past. The surroundings get rougher as they drive down the road 'til they get to the turning circle at the end, where the driver pulls up next to the burnt-out Astra. The Hezbollah would feel at home.

Whacko gets out and approaches the end block which contains upstairs and downstairs flats accessed by a communal door. The block is one of those that doesn't have a number but a name; in this case it was Silver Cross, after the rusting wheel-less pram hiding in the front garden, camouflaged by foot-high grass and dandelions. Jonno, (the man who owes the money) lives in an upstairs flat, the front elevation comprising 3 windows in one casement. Jonno (or maybe a friend of Jonno's, or perhaps someone who can't stand Jonno) had updated this arrangement into two pieces of plywood and one window with a tatty curtain permanently pulled across.

The communal door which led to upstairs and downstairs flat was half and half. Top half plywood bottom half reinforced glass.

The whacko shouts at the top of his voice. (8:45 am Tuesday school day remember)

"Jonno you cunt, get yer fuckin arse down here now"

Mums walking with children on the way to school don't quite know where to put their faces, and as the air turns blue the driver turns crimson.

A few seconds pass and whack job is revving up to bellow again when Jonno thankfully pokes his dishevelled head out of the only working window.

"Hang on for fucks sake, will yer."

It seems Jonno doesn't want to be outdone in the industrial language stakes.

Eventually Jonno lets whacko in and the driver exchanges small talk with whack jobs tree hugging companion as she gets out to smoke a spliff.

2 minutes later Whacko emerges and from up his sleeve he produces two, foot long bread knives. Jonno comes out behind him shrugging his shoulders at Joan Baez. The driver's eyes widened but Joan had had so much booze and pot her eyes couldn't manage it.

Whacko marches purposefully down the street (to visit his sister one presumes) and his companion, sensing something is about to happen moans softly "oh no" just as the sound of tinkling glass can be heard from 50 yards up the street.

The driver takes this as his cue to leave, thanks the taxi gods again that he's already got a 20 spot and bids a fond farewell to the spliff smoker. As he drives slowly past, he sees whacko removing the wheelie bin he's just thrown through somebody's front window, and proceeds to smash the shards away with his two breadknives, all the time imploring the terrified, screaming, pyjama wearing occupants to open the now redundant front fuckin door. Sensibly they refused, and continued screaming like banshees as whacko ranted and raved on their front garden waving his knives about. Meanwhile, his laid-back companion looked on like it was an everyday occurrence. (Who knows, to her it may well have been)

As the driver makes his way back to

civilisation, umpteen police cars, sirens

blaring race past him and he breathes a huge

sigh of relief. He'll remember those two

that's for sure.

RUNNERS.

Every cabbie at some time has had a punter do a runner.

Whether chase is given depends on the cabbie's girth, the punter that's just legged it, and of course, how much it matters to said cabbie. It's always irksome but is it worth a heart attack?

Well, it was to Jimmy Opal. Rational thought went out the window and Jimmy went out the door when his punter absconded. Jimmy was out like a flash and giving chase.

Left then right then right then right again.
The runner seemed to know the area well,
another quick left, then right, then right again
and as Jimmy came puffing round the corner,
he spotted the bastard jumping into a car. Oh
FFS. That car looks familiar. Oh dear. In his
haste he'd left the keys in the ignition. Jimmy
felt a bit of a dick as his taxi roared off into
the sunset.

A different day, and a different punter
with his mate, little bit thicker than your
average runners.

They leap out and scarper down an alleyway giving the bemused driver the bunny's ears as they go.

The driver takes a pragmatic view and allows himself a rueful smile.

The thick bastards have forgotten they put a crate of booze in the boot worth 5 times the fare.

PRAMS.

Prams, buggies, strollers, push-chairs, trollies, call 'em what you will, ladies and gentlemen they are a necessary evil.

When demonstrated in the shop by an assistant with a degree in mechanical engineering (Pram division) they seem like a good idea. How ingenious that at the lightest touch of a lever or button the whole thing collapses beautifully into an almost flat self-locking bundle that is both easily manoeuvrable and surprisingly light.

Now add the following:

Mum, 20 years old tops. In her best JLS onesie, fluffy, bunny eared ankle slippers, and pink dressing gown, an I-phone glued to her ear, trying to roll a ciggie and open a can of Red Bull at the same time. Three kids, all with snotty snitches, and two with sagging nappies, are ignoring her because she's ignoring them. She breaks off her call to Donna momentarily (she was only calling her a slapper anyway) to cajole (swear at) the kids into getting in the taxi whilst the driver swears at the pram, with rain, dripping down his arse-crack.

A rain cover (Not properly attached) designed to not bend when you want it too, a bit like that cardboard box at Christmas that never collapses when you stand and jump on it spraining your ankle in the process.

A foot-muff. Contained unseen within the foot muff, fourteen half-eaten, mashed by a toddler Gregg's sausage rolls. In the string bag hung below the pram resides the following: 10 scratched losing scratch cards, 16 empty Wotsits packets (obviously mum's favourite) an empty Pringles canister. One partly sucked, sticky party ring biscuit (stuck to the netting). An open packet of custard creams crushed to smithereens, which spill crumbs out liberally all over the boot. An opened pack of baby wipes (fully dried out and useless) A nappy (unsoiled thank god) the woman's handbag which feels like it's got two house bricks in it, and a bottle of Lambrini.

The fun doesn't end there though. On the pram handles, £50's worth of shopping in 4 plastic bags, the straining handles of which snap when the driver tries to take them off to load the pram in, and last but not least last year's trip to Benidorm, Alicante airport baggage label.

Now, *you* try and fold that fucker flat!

GET OUT!

Under normal circumstances the one thing you can be sure of in taxiing is that sooner or later the punter is going to get out. Usually when they reach their destination, and they generally don't dawdle too much in case the meter ticks over.

However, as you've probably guessed there is always one who wants to be awkward. He only did it once mind.

For no apparent reason other than the

desire to be a nuisance, said punter decides one boring Tuesday afternoon that he quite likes it in the back of Oscar's Octavia and he's not going to get out when they reach their destination, but stay there all afternoon, riding about and sight-seeing. He's taking root. Oscar naturally points out that the meter is still running and that every minute is costing the awkward git more bugs.

The punter shrugs his shoulders and the driver has a feeling that getting the dosh might be harder than getting him out.

Oscar contemplates manhandling the geezer and pulling him out, but that's easier said than done as the punter's a bit of a fat bastard, and probably thinks he is Rocky Balboa.

Oscar decides to radio the office and speak to Dave, known as the professor, who as luck would have it, is on the desk. He's known as the professor because he talks posh and has been to Uni, or is a lecturer or something, and that's all it takes to be considered a professor of something, to your run of the mill, hairy arsed, thick as they come cabbie.

"Bring him to the office Oscar, I'll shift him for yer" said the prof.

Oscar smiled and looked at the smug punter through his rear-view mirror. He'd heard every word and didn't seem unduly worried; in fact, a look of relish came across his un-bruised, non-bleeding, countenance.

That would soon change.

Back at the office, Oscar pulls up on the car park and the professor jogs out to meet him. The customer snorts and gives a little laugh as if to say "Is that it! *He's* gunna shift *me,* is he?" There must have been a bit of underlying tension that he was hiding though, because the relief had made his bowels loosen a bit and he treated the driver to a long slow satisfying fart.

The professor was not very tall, or muscular looking, not very intimidating at all really, in fact he looked like a smaller, skinnier version of shaggy out of Scooby Do.

That's where the similarities ended though, and if the punter had known about the professor he would have been out of the car like greased lightning.

You see, although the professor was mid-forties and benign looking, he was in fact ex-military. Special forces in fact and not scared of anything, or, anyone. Trained in Krav Maga amongst other combat techniques, wiry and strong as an ox under the baggy scruffy clothing, he was quite simply a completely unafraid, very hard, man.

Since he left the military, he had lived the quiet life as a taxi shift operator amongst other things and didn't brag about his past.

The professor opens the rear door and asks the customer nicely if he'll please get out. He didn't comply so the professor, with astonishing speed, punched him three times, blackening his eye, bursting his lip, and loosening a few teeth.

The Prof asked him again and lo and behold this time he got out! Fancy that! Would you believe it, that's all it took to make him see sense?

"What does he owe you Oscar?" asks the prof, giving the customer a chance to gather himself

"Seven quid" says Oscar.

The Professor being a man of honour asked the punter for £10. He says the extra is for the inconvenience and the disgusting smell. Mr awkward paid up, not a murmur out of him, mainly because he was still gingerly waggling his front teeth, and dabbing his snout.

The moral of the story? Don't piss the driver off by being an awkward git. Pay up, get out, bon voyage.

THE LONG LIST.

This story wouldn't be half as entertaining (it wouldn't be entertaining at all because nothing would have gone wrong) if:
A) Roy hadn't got the job.

And B) He wasn't a complete technophobe and didn't have a mobile phone. (They were still in their infancy)

The long list is not a long list but a list of long jobs. In rotation drivers get a stab at a long job as they come up. Usually anything over 30 miles is considered a long job and if you're unlucky you wait twelve months and then get a thirty quid job to Bolton which is shite.

On this particular occasion the job is to London; overnight stop and return. Plumsters. Plummington. Plummerooney. As plummy as they get really, a regular customer too! A business woman who has an annual meeting.

They operator looks at the list to see which lucky driver is next and groans. Roy Tango is next, and she toys immediately with bypassing him, but she knows that he knows that he knows he's next and will kick off if

he's overlooked for such a plum job.

The problem is…….. well, its Roy. He's

the problem. He gets lost on local jobs, can

never find a pick up, forgets where the pick-

up is on the way to the pick-up and is

constantly on the airwaves asking for

reminders. Operators constantly give him half

decent local jobs just to keep him busy for

half an hour so he's not on the fuckin radio

mithering them.

Roy is informed of the job which is the

day after tomorrow, 5am start. He's cock-ahoop and why not. The operators would normally throw a party to be rid of Roy for two days but everybody knows there's an almighty fuck up looming.

Through a stroke of unbelievable bad luck, Roy picks up the business woman the day before the biggie on a school run and asks her if his 10-year-old daughter can ride shotgun on the journey. He'll show her round London coz she's never been and it'll be educational for her. The woman (a mum herself) being put in a bit of a spot and a

kindly soul and against her better judgement
agrees.

All seems well on the journey down.
They arrive in time and Roy's not got lost
and his daughter is quiet and pleasant enough
so everybody's happy.

"See you tomorrow at 11am" Roy
breezily announces as he retrieves the lady's
case from the boot of his car and off she trots.

A lovely sightseeing day and evening in
London ensues for Roy and his daughter after
they've dumped their gear in their budget
digs which are miles out of central London.

Up early at 07:30 so as not to be late and set off in plenty of time for the return pick up.

Now, what was the name of that fuckin hotel? And what's more, where the fuck is it? His brow is furrowing and his sweat glands are going into overdrive, as he mutters to himself "shit, shit, shit"

He cruises round London for 2 hours trying to find the hotel where his customer will be waiting. His daughter, trying to help, keeps repeating "Are yer fuckin lost dad?" which doesn't help. He's not daft though is our Roy (well he is a bit) so eventually he finds a call box and rings the office in Manchester asking for directions!!!

They give him the name of the hotel which is a help but directions from 250 miles away seems a bit of a stretch. He stops frequently and asks pedestrians by the bucketful but none of them are from London! How can that be? back home everybody is local!

Time goes by and an ever more frantic Roy, his stomach churning, is coming apart at the seams. His daughter's "are yer *still* fuckin lost dad?" mantra is starting to get on his FUCKIN' NERVES.

Eventually at 11:30 Roy accepts defeat. The Thames looks inviting. He rings the office to be told his extremely irate customer has jumped in a black cab and is halfway up the M1. The fare, which will be eye-watering, is to be borne by Roy on his return. He can imagine the meter, resembling a fruit machine as the miles race by under the tyres. The Thames *really* looks inviting. He'd throw himself in but he can't swim.

Dejected, he starts the long journey home.

His daughter has the good sense to keep her

trap shut all the way which is a feat.

So, in the final analysis he's missed two

day's work, spent a fortune on an overnight

stop and London's tourist attractions, bought 300 ice-creams, 40 hot dogs, and a souvenir from every fuckin attraction. He's fuelled up 3 times for fuck all, incurred a yet unknown massive bill, pissed off a regular customer to the point where she's mentioned compo, and hates his daughter. But she's not too keen on him either at the mo so they're square.

ΠΟWT ΤΟ SEE.

Despite what you might think dear reader, most journeys are dull, uneventful affairs.

A conversation about dull uneventful journeys was taking place during a dull, uneventful journey on a midweek trip around lunch-time, and the punter remarked as they passed through Ancoats, Manchester, how dull and uneventful Manchester was; grimy, dilapidated, with nowt to see. The driver naturally agreed as he did with everything every punter ever said. At that point driver and punter, as if to confirm to themselves and each other the truth of the statement, glanced to their left down a cobbled side street, no different to the dozen's they'd already passed.

And there before them was a man, doing something.

He was smartly dressed in a business suit, shirt and tie. Now dear reader before the big reveal on the next page I'd like you to take a few seconds to try a guess what they saw the man doing. I guarantee you will not guess it correctly unless you cheat or, you actually are that business man, or the passenger, or his best mate, or his mum or dad, coz he will have told them. Perhaps his girlfriend too but you get my drift.

Please turn to the next page to find out………..

He was riding a UNICYCLE!!

"Well, apart from that of course" said the punter smiling.

THE END.

Now dear reader we've reached the end of our shift and it's time for bed.

But next time you're in the back of an Octavia, or a black cab, or a minibus, spare a thought for the geezer behind the wheel. He's going about his business, just trying to make a living like the rest of us, and now you have an insight as to what he might have been through.

Try if you can to say those three little words, we all long to hear, you know the ones.

"Keep the change"

Keep saying it like a mantra.

"Keep the change, keep the change"

It'll cheer the driver up no end because you never know he might be the one who took a dead dog to the vets or, the one with a rubber mallet in his door pocket. Check his 'earole in case it's got dog shit in it. If he's grimacing a lot and doesn't want to chat it's probably because he's dying for a shit and he's concentrating really hard on not soiling himself.

Anyway, whatever you do, really try your hardest **_to_** ask, have you read 'Ave yer bin Busy? And if they haven't, well you know what to do. By the way don't forget the tip.

A hefty one if you please. Thanks.

ACKNOWLEDGEMENTS

First of all, to the Operators because if I don't give

them first mention I'll be punished.

Thanks also to the customers, mainly for

paying me and providing fodder for the stories.

Last but not least my colleagues for supplying

tales not experienced by myself.

A special mention to Millie Harrop, what a

talent! She makes things come alive.

Millie can be reached at snail.art@aol.co.uk

Or, at snailishart on Instagram

ABOUT THE AUTHOR

Simon Whiskey has written all sorts of other stuff, including a sit-com, a farce, a musical, seventy plus songs, and 7 children's stories, none of which have seen the light of day.

He's also invented a card game, and three board games. They haven't either.

He's read loads of books, and Viz, and is also a card, wit, and good egg.

You can contact him via Twitter @SimonWhiskey

Printed in Great Britain
by Amazon